REMBRANDT

Elizabeth Elias Kaufman

Minster Books

CONTENTS

COLOR ILLUSTRATIONS

REMBRANDT

Rembrandt is the acknowledged master painter and etcher of the Baroque era. Few artists have ever equaled his ability to use light. He experienced the fate of most great artists in reverse. Recognized as a genius early in life, his popularity and fortune gradually disappeared. Bankruptcy was the least of the tragedies he faced. However, if ever there was an indomitable artistic spirit, it belonged to Rembrandt. His personal problems only seemed to strengthen his ability to portray the human character.

Although his early work had been acclaimed, his mature pieces were not understood; for in his later years, Rembrandt's art was at odds with the prevailing public taste. To understand how this happened, it is helpful to examine art in the seventeenth century.

HIS TIMES

Baroque is the term given to the majority of art produced in Europe during the seventeenth century. The term comes from the word jewelers used to describe a large, imperfect pearl. Thus, originally the term was used in a rather derogatory sense.

At the end of the High Renaissance, a new style developed known as Mannerism. Works produced in this period tend to be artificial and affected. One of the most famous examples of Mannerism is Parmigianino's *The Madonna with the Long Neck*. Painted in 1535, the work exhibits the languid elongation characteristic of art produced at the time.

The development of Mannerism was the result of two conditions. The High Renaissance had been a curious period. It lasted for a very brief span of time. There were only a handful of masters and even fewer minor artists. The works created by men such as Michelangelo and Leonardo da Vinci could not be improved upon. Although their styles and techniques could be taught to talented followers, the spark that defined their genius could not be transmitted to the next generation of artists. Consequently, these new artists developed their own style, based on the work produced during the High Renaissance.

The other condition that led to Mannerism was the Reformation. The first reaction of the Catholic Church was to retrench. The Council of Trent produced a reactionary climate. As time went by, Mannerism became more inflexible, paralleling changes in the Church.

The development of Baroque art is more difficult to explain. One of the most important influences was the Counter Reformation. This was especially true in Italy, where the style originated. In other countries, there were other reasons. However, as had been true since the Early Renaissance, what began in Italy quickly spread to other European countries.

The Catholic Church resumed the patronage of the arts begun during the High Renaissance. Among the many artists who came to Rome in response to the new opportunities were Caravaggio and Carracci. These two men are usually considered to be the first Baroque artists. The work they produced was a dramatic change from the Mannerist style.

Baroque art represents a reunion of art and nature. Artists were not so concerned with intellectuality. They were more interested in displaying spiritualism in human terms. Thus, their spiritual appeal was through the senses rather than the intellect. This philosophy produced highly emotional works.

The theatrical nature of Baroque art is its most obvious characteristic. Several techniques were used to develop this effect. Art created during the High Renaissance was often based on the triangle or pyramid. Mannerist artists continued this tradition. However, Baroque art was more often asymmetrical. Diagonal lines were frequently employed to add tension. In conjunction with a change in geometric shape, there was a change in the treatment of light and darkness. Previously, chiaroscuro (the interplay of light and shade) was used to model and form the subject. Baroque art used the effects of light in a different fashion. Shadows took on dramatic purpose, often being used to establish the illusion of tremendous spatial depth. Additionally, Baroque art was usually fairly realistic. The affectation of Mannerism was abandoned, but so was the idealized type associated with the High Renaissance.

As Baroque art spread to other countries, it was modified by existing conditions. Holland was a nation of Protestants. Thus, much of the religious art produced in other parts of Europe never flourished in the northern Netherlands.

During the first half of the seventeenth century, Holland was involved in several wars. After the treaties were signed, the country was free from French and Spanish domination. As a result of trade and hard work, the citizens of Holland enjoyed a fairly high standard of living. A large middle class developed.

Members of the middle class, the burghers, were enthusiastic art patrons. However, a practical nation demanded practical, realistic art. Paintings were required to look like life. The sensible burghers were not interested in flights of fancy, deep meanings, or spiritual reinforcement in their art. Works which employed religious subjects such as Rembrandt's **St. Paul in Prison** (plate 4) had to be personal and individual rather than being idealized.

What the burghers particularly favored was portraiture, especially the group portrait. Civic guards, aldermen, university faculties, and guilds were all clamoring to be immortalized in oils. Among others, Rembrandt painted group portraits for the medical school. One such is **The Anatomy Lesson of Dr. Joan Deyman** (plate 41).

Artists who managed to master the group portrait as well as other realistic subjects were financially successful. However, an artist whose works were not attuned to the public taste had no other place to turn to market his art. Unlike France, with its ruling Fine Arts Academy, Holland had no critical central art body. Holland in the seventeenth century was one of the few places where people rather than institutions dictated public tastes. This is not to say that an artist had a wider range of tastes to which he could appeal. The burghers in Holland had remarkably similar tastes.

Finally, because of its relative religious tolerance, Holland attracted a wide variety of people from other countries. Many Protestants and Jews came to Holland to escape the religious persecution so prevalent in Europe at the time. This influx of different people provided an artist such as Rembrandt with a wealth of subjects for his paintings. In portraying religious scenes, Rembrandt frequently used Jews as models. This was a novel idea at the time.

HIS LIFE

Rembrandt Harmenszoon van Rijn was born on July 15, 1606 in Leiden. Authorities differ on the number of his siblings. Some claim he was the seventh of eight children; others that he was the eighth of nine children. It is likely that the confusion is the result of the early death of one or more of his siblings.

The artist's background has frequently been romanticized. His family is often described as impoverished. In fact, Rembrandt came from solid middle class stock. His father, Harmen Gerritszoon van Rijn (van Rijn indicated that the family lived near the Rhine River), was a miller. His mother, Neeltge van

Zuytbrouck, was the daughter of a baker. Although not rich, the couple could well afford to raise their large family.

Rembrandt's education began at the Leiden Latin School. In 1620, at the age of fourteen, he was admitted to the University of Leiden, at that time one of the strongest centers of scholarship in Europe. However, Rembrandt's primary interest was in art, not books. Within a few months after entering the university, he left.

Unlike many artists, Rembrandt did not have to fight his family in order to pursue his career. The great interest in art in Holland provided an excellent climate for artists. In any event, his natural talents were recognized and encouraged by his family. After dropping out of the University of Leiden, Rembrandt was apprenticed to Jacob van Swanenburgh, a local artist. Although he studied with Swanenburgh for three years, the man made little impression on Rembrandt's style.

With his father's support, Rembrandt next went to Amsterdam to study under Pieter Lastman who, like Swanenburgh, had studied in Italy. Lastman was one of the leading artists in Holland. From him, Rembrandt learned the elements of the Baroque style including the importance and various uses of chiaroscuro (the interplay of light and dark). Although he stayed in Amsterdam only six months, Rembrandt was strongly influenced by Lastman.

By 1624 or 1625, Rembrandt had returned to Leiden as an independent artist with his own studio. At about this time, he became acquainted with another young artist, Jan Lievens, who had also studied in Amsterdam with Lastman. It is possible that for a while they shared the same studio. At this point in their careers, the work they produced was very similar. The inference is that there was a degree of collaboration.

Lievens was important in Rembrandt's life because it was through this second artist that Rembrandt met Constantyn Huygens, an important government official and art patron. Huygens helped Rembrandt at the time as well as later in the artist's career. This original success was probably responsible for Rembrandt's move from Leiden back to Amsterdam in 1631 or 1632.

Amsterdam was an important commercial center with a major port. It was well on the way to becoming a leading center for the arts. When Rembrandt arrived in Amsterdam, there was a demand for portrait painters. The artist was quick to oblige.

His first group portrait, *The Anatomy Lesson of Dr. Tulp,* painted in 1632, established his reputation. Thereafter, Rembrandt painted a number of group portraits. He also began doing fashionable portraits such as the *Portrait of Maurits Huygens* (plate 11), the brother of Constantyn Huygens. At the same time, he continued painting Biblical scenes such as *The Sacrifice of Isaac* (plate 19), executed in 1636.

When Rembrandt moved back to Amsterdam, he lived in the home of Hendrick van Uhlenburgh, an art dealer. In 1634, Rembrandt married Saskia van Uhlenburgh, Hendrick's niece. Her family belonged to the upper class. Thus, although there is no doubt that Rembrandt truly loved Saskia, the marriage gave him financial security as well as a certain social standing.

Rembrandt frequently used his wife as his model. In addition to painting several portraits of her such as *Saskia van Uhlenburgh, Wife of the Artist* (plate 14), she appears in many paintings as a character.

With Saskia's help and his own financial success, Rembrandt bought a new home. His happiness and contentment did not last. Saskia bore four children. Only one, Titus, lived past infancy. In 1642, a year after the birth of Titus, Saskia died.

In the same year Saskia died, Rembrandt painted the famous *Night Watch,* a group portrait of a militia. There is a persistent belief that this painting was responsible for Rembrandt's financial problems. This was not the case. There is no evidence to prove that the *Night Watch* was not acceptable to its sponsors, the militiamen.

It is true that beginning in 1642, Rembrandt was less successful in selling his work. However, his problems stemmed more from changing public tastes than from an unfavorable reaction to any one piece of art. Rembrandt's style and the public taste were moving in opposite directions. The public wanted exciting Baroque art. Rembrandt was moving beyond pure Baroque, producing deeper, more meaningful works.

The death of Saskia affected Rembrandt financially as well as emotionally. The terms of her will inadvertently prevented him from remarrying. At the time her will was written, Rembrandt was very successful. There was no reason to believe that his fortunes would change. Saskia's will stipulated that should the artist remarry, her estate would pass on to her sister. As his popularity waned, his income diminished to the point where the loss of income from Saskia's estate was unacceptable to him.

As a result, Rembrandt was forced to hire a succession of housekeepers to manage his home and care for his son. Finally, he hired *Hendrickje Stoffels* (plate 26). She lived with him for approximately twenty years serving first as housekeeper, then model, and eventually as his mistress.

By the late 1650's, Rembrandt's financial situation had deteriorated to the point where he was bankrupt. His mistress and son rescued him by establishing a corporation and hiring Rembrandt as an employee.

Although he was still receiving commissions for his work, the last years of his life were filled with personal misfortunes. Hendrickje died in 1663. His son Titus died shortly after his own marriage in 1668. Rembrandt, the genius of his age, died on October 4, 1669. He was sixty-three.

HIS WORKS

PLATE 1

The Angel and the Prophet Balaam was painted in 1626, when Rembrandt was twenty years old. The work is based on the Biblical story told in Numbers XVII. It was illustrated in the dramatic style the artist had learned from Pieter Lastman. *The Angel and the Prophet Balaam* is a typically Baroque painting without the technical and esthetic finesse Rembrandt acquired later in his career. In his finest works, Rembrandt's use of light is unexcelled by any other artist. Here, however, the lighting is blatant and harsh. It strikes the three principal characters (the angel, the ass, and Balaam) with the same intensity. The riders and the one horse that is visible are seen in an unconvincing half-light. The two figures on the right of Balaam are in shade.

PLATE 2

Rembrandt found the inspiration for *Tobit and Anna with the Kid* in the Apocrypha. Tobit was a good and wise man who became blind after doing a good deed. When Anna brings home a kid that was given to her, Tobit accuses her of stealing it. Although this is an early work, painted in the same year as *The Angel and the Prophet Balaam* (plate 1), the artist was already displaying his ability to accurately portray human emotions. The old man is grieving what he thinks is a theft while his wife shows her shock at being falsely accused. It is believed that Rembrandt used his mother as the model for Anna.

PLATE 3

The most impressive aspect of the *Flight into Egypt* is the dramatic lighting. Painted in the period between 1625 and 1626, *Flight into Egypt* is an excellent example of the powerful use of chiaroscuro (the interplay of light and dark). However, the piece lacks subtlety. Part of the problem stems from the fact that the single source of lights seems centered on the ground. The halo around the Christ Child appears to be more of a fire than a halo. Approximately a quarter of a century later, Rembrandt etched this same theme. In that later work, he displays a more mature talent.

PLATE 4

St. Paul in Prison was painted in 1627. Even at that early stage in his career, Rembrandt was using light in inventive ways. Notice that the light that illuminates St. Paul is coming from the window. That in itself is not unusual. However, the light does not stop once it strikes the face, it is reflected on the background wall. Another characteristic of Rembrandt's style that is evident here is his remarkable attention to detail. The folds of drapery, the pages of the manuscript, and even the shoes have been executed with care.

PLATE 5

In this *Self-Portrait*, painted in about 1628, Rembrandt appears to have been working on the effects of lighting. The angle of the light source leaves the face in shadow, almost totally obscuring the features. The tone of the painting, the wild mop of hair, and the brooding quality developed through the use of lighting provide a stark contrast to two other self-portraits the artist painted approximately one year later. In the later portraits (plates 7, 9), the lighting is applied in an entirely different fashion for an entirely different purpose.

PLATE 6

Rembrandt reveals his narrative talents in *Christ at Emmaus*. The story is from Luke. Christ has traveled with two strangers. After blessing the bread, Christ is suddenly revealed to them. As was the case with Leonardo's *Last Supper*, Rembrandt chose the most dramatic moment. The man facing the viewer is consumed with fear and awe. The other man kneels in front of Christ, his overturned chair behind him. The theatrical lighting has no obvious source; it is part of the miraculous revelation. In later years, Rembrandt created another painting using the same theme. The second version, painted in 1648, is less theatrical and more spiritual.

PLATE 7

This *Self-Portrait* shows Rembrandt as an intelligent, self-confident young man. Painted in about 1629, it lacks the depth that many of his later works display. Nevertheless, it is one of the first self-portraits in which Rembrandt attempted to reflect his personality on canvas. The artist had a fondness for armour. In later years, he would own a collection of it.

The light source for this painting originates from the left. Because of the angle of the lighting the work gives the impression of being a profile. Notice how he used the light to help define the armour around the neck.

PLATE 8

In 1629, Rembrandt painted this piece known as *The Tribute Money.* One of the interesting elements in the work is the architecture. The artist used it to frame and enhance the main subject of the piece. Christ stands in front of a column that helps draw the viewer's eye to the halo. Notice that the light strikes the subjects facing Christ, but fades rapidly behind Christ. There, the entire right-hand side of the painting is in shadow (including the figure in the balcony window). The figure on the stairs watching the scene is seen in a half-light.

PLATE 9

As he did in many of his self-portraits, Rembrandt painted himself bedecked in finery in this *Self-Portrait* from 1629. The careful attention to detail is obvious in the clothes and hair and is extraordinary in the bejeweled hat and feather. In the same year that this work was painted, Rembrandt was visited by

Constantyn Huygens, an important government official and art patron. Huygens was very favorably impressed with Rembrandt's work. It is possible that this romanticized *Self-Portrait* was executed as a display of his ego following Huygens flattery. In any event, the dramatic lighting is in contrast with the more subtle lighting he used in his later works.

PLATE 10

Jeremiah Contemplating the Destruction of Jerusalem is one of the masterpieces of Rembrandt's youth. Unlike *St. Paul in Prison* (plate 4), there is little artifice. Where *St. Paul in Prison* is theatrical, this work is subtle. The emotion in both pieces is powerful, but in this painting, it has a stronger effect on the viewer.

The figure and his surroundings are carefully blended. Throughout his career, Rembrandt was interested in men in contemplative poses. The head-on-hand pose is very effective in creating a psychological mood here. The light source is to the right, where Jerusalem burns. Rembrandt has established a dramatic contrast between the fire and ruins of Jeremiah's beloved Jerusalem and his richly appointed attire. The artist plays on this contrast by adding the few treasures Jeremiah has saved. They glitter in the reflected light.

PLATE 11

In 1632, shortly after he moved to Amsterdam, Rembrandt was asked to paint the *Portrait of Maurits Huygens,* the older brother of Constantyn Huygens. The commission was a result of the visit Constantyn had made to Rembrandt's Leiden studio. The subject is wearing a fancy lace collar. This Dutch fashion appears in most portraits produced at the time.

PLATE 12

The painting known as *The Artist's Sister* is considered by experts to be a portrait of

Rembrandt's sister, Liesbeth. The work was painted in 1632. In the same year, Rembrandt painted another portrait of what is believed to be the same woman. The second portrait is in profile. In both paintings, the subject has a double chin. Although most authorities believe that both portraits are of Liesbeth, a few scholars maintain that the model for the paintings was Saskia. Their theory is supported by a portrait of Saskia (*Saskia with a Hat*) painted in about 1633. Saskia's profile is remarkably similar (including the double chin) to the profile portrait of Liesbeth.

PLATE 13

The success of Rembrandt's *The Anatomy Lesson of Dr. Tulp* led to a long string of portrait commissions. A number of these were group portraits. However, the majority of Rembrandt's portraits were for single subjects. This *Portrait of Maarten Looten* is typical of the portrait work Rembrandt produced during his first few years in Amsterdam.

Looten was a wealthy merchant. He is shown in a pleasant pose, holding a letter. Like Looten, most of Rembrandt's subjects were burghers, members of the middle class.

PLATE 14

In 1633, Rembrandt became engaged to Saskia. *Saskia van Uhlenburgh, Wife of the Artist* was painted between 1633 and 1635. The subject has been posed and painted with a very demure expression. In later portraits, Saskia appears to be more of a matron. In fact, Rembrandt frequently used his wife as a model for female characters.

PLATE 15

The *Portrait of the Reverend Johannes Elison* was painted in 1634. This piece and a portrait of the Reverend's wife were commissioned by the couple's son. The family lived in Norwich, England, but they visited Amster-

dam several times. During one such visit, Rembrandt painted the two portraits. This is one of Rembrandt's best portraits from his early years in Amsterdam. While it lacks the depth his later portraits have, it shows his interest in the human character. The subject is clothed in full clerical garb, sitting on an imposing chair. The chair itself has not been handled as well as the props on the table.

PLATE 16

Rembrandt and Saskia were married in 1634. In that same year, he painted this *Self-Portrait*. The pose and finery suggest that this might have been painted at the time of his marriage. The fancy hat is almost a Rembrandt trademark. He frequently included hats in his self-portraits. Rembrandt was always self conscious of his nose. Here it is slightly exaggerated to give it extra prominence.

Most of the portraits he was painting at this time involved the wealthy middle class. Standard fashionable dress for them was a black coat and white lace collar. Notice that Rembrandt does not dress himself this way. In fact, he seems to have made a point of giving the entire work an aristocratic touch.

PLATE 17

The double portrait, *Rembrandt and Saskia,* is one of the artist's most famous paintings. Yet within the context of Rembrandt's work, it is a somewhat strange piece. At the time it was painted, Rembrandt was producing fairly somber works. The coarse and boisterous nature of the painting is at odds with his other works.

The portrait shows Saskia posed on Rembrandt's knee. The artist is portrayed as a swashbuckling cavalier; she, as a somewhat more refined lady. The raised glass of wine, the pheasant on the table, and the detail in general imply the scene is a tavern or inn.

There are several theories to explain this unique piece. One states the obvious, that Rembrandt was ecstatic about his marriage.

Another is a variation on this theme; that the two faces, one showing restraint, the other, exuberance, represent the difference in their natures. However, this painting is also known as **The Prodigal Son in a Tavern.** Dutch art often showed a laughing man with an attractive woman perched on his lap to represent part of the Biblical story of the Prodigal Son. Thus, the third theory is that Rembrandt did not mean to have this piece taken at its face value.

PLATE 18

Although Rembrandt did not produce many landscape paintings, the ones he created are masterpieces. **Landscape with the Baptism of Chamberlain** is an example of the type of landscape he painted during the latter part of the 1630's. The scene is imaginary. It bears no real relationship to the flat Dutch countryside. Few of his landscapes are devoid of humanity. In this case, the baptism takes place in the foreground. The area in which the action occurs represents less than ten percent of the entire work.

PLATE 19

The Sacrifice of Isaac shows the artist's incredible story-telling abilities. The theme is the Biblical story of how God tested Abraham. Abraham was told to take his only son, Isaac, to a far off mountain. There, Abraham was to bind Isaac, lay him on a pile of wood, and offer him as a sacrifice to God. As Abraham is about to slay his beloved son, an angel of the Lord stops him. Behind him, Abraham found a ram, caught by its horns in a thicket. The ram was offered in place of his son.

Rembrandt has painted the dramatic moment when the angel intervenes. Each element of the story is present. Isaac rests on a pile of wood, his hands bound behind him. His father's hand rests on his face, exposing his neck and sparing him from witnessing what is about to happen. The force of the angel's grip on Abraham's arm has released the knife. The ram can be seen in the background of the painting.

There are two very similar versions of this painting. The one illustrated here is a copy of the original painted by one of Rembrandt's students. An inscription indicates that Rembrandt supervised the work and made corrections.

PLATE 20

The rough work known as **Joseph Relating His Dreams** is believed to have been executed in preparation for an etching created about a year later in 1638. Unlike **The Sacrifice of Isaac** (plate 19), this piece does not attempt to freeze the action at the most dramatic moment. Instead, Rembrandt gives the viewer an opportunity to witness reactions. Joseph stands in front of his seated father. His mother leans forward, dividing her attention between Joseph's earnest speech and his father's quiet skepticism. Behind Joseph, his brothers react in different ways.

PLATE 21

Rembrandt used the Biblical character of Samson in quite a few of his works. The painting, **Samson's Wedding Feast,** is probably the most famous of these. Even at the time it was recognized as a masterpiece. As was the case with all of his Biblical scenes, the painting accurately portrays the Scriptural story. Samson, seated next to his Philistine bride, is posing a riddle to several of the guests. It is believed that the figure holding the flute (behind Samson) is Rembrandt's self-portrait.

PLATE 22

The artist continued to be much in demand as a portrait painter. In 1639, he painted the **Portrait of Maria Trip,** also known as **A Young Woman of Quality.** Rembrandt had painted portraits of other members of her family. In this piece, he has chosen to emphasize the richness of her costume, accentuated with fine jewelry. The style of the dress is more provocative than normal. The detail work on the lace and jewelry is very fine.

PLATE 23

In 1640, Rembrandt painted *The Meeting Between Mary and Elizabeth,* also known as *The Visitation.* The scene depicts Mary's arrival. Elizabeth, six months pregnant, greets her. Her husband, Zacharias, old and bent, is just coming through the door. Elizabeth's face indicates that she realizes Mary's importance.

In the foreground are several symbolic birds. To the right in the background, Rembrandt depicts part of Jerusalem. The detail work on the house is an example of Rembrandt's skill in using architecture to enhance the picture.

PLATE 24

Manoah's Sacrifice, also known as *Manoah's Offering,* is one of Rembrandt's best works. The painting was inspired by the story in the Book of Judges about Samson's parents. Manoah's barren wife is told by an angel in the shape of a man that she will have a son. Manoah asks that God return the angel to confirm the story. Rembrandt's painting shows the angel ascending to heaven after the second visit. In conformance with the Biblical description, the angel has no wings. Manoah and his wife, having made a burnt offering, are shown in prayer.

By this point in his career, Rembrandt had changed his emphasis. No longer content to merely tell a story, he focuses on the human character and its internal reaction to God's intervention. Much of the drama present in Rembrandt's earlier work is gone, replaced with a deeper spirituality. This change represents his artistic growth and departure from pure Baroque.

PLATE 25

This *Portrait of a Man,* painted in 1641, is believed to be a portrait of Nicolaas van Bambeeck. The man's clothes, hat, and lace collar indicate that he was a burgher, a member of the wealthy middle class. The angle of the light that strikes his face leaves half of his features in shadow.

PLATE 26

After Saskia died in 1642, Rembrandt hired several housekeepers to help him and to take care of his young son, Titus. *Hendrickje Stoffels* was one of these. She became his model and eventually his mistress. There is little doubt that Rembrandt would have married her except for the conditions of Saskia's will. Although not meant to keep him from remarrying, the conditions would have financially ruined him had he done so. When his financial situation worsened, he had no choice but to remain single.

The painting shows a simple woman dressed in a seductive costume that is unlike anything Saskia posed in. The difference in clothing symbolizes the difference in personalities. Hendrickje had none of Saskia's sophisticated polish. In fact, Hendrickje could neither read nor write.

PLATE 27

The tenderness apparent in *Manoah's Sacrifice* (plate 24) is also present in *Young Girl Leaning on a Windowsill.* The work is suffused with charm, tenderness, and love. The model for this painting is not known. It could not be either Hendrickje or her daughter because of the age discrepancy. However, Rembrandt's feeling for children is very obvious in this piece.

The detail work and treatment of light is truly beautiful. There is a softness in this painting that is characteristic of Rembrandt's mature style.

PLATE 28

The painting known as *Woman in Bed* is difficult to date. Most art scholars only agree that it was painted sometime between 1645 and 1650. Saskia had died in 1642. By the time *Woman in Bed* was painted, Hendrickje Stoffels was living with Rembrandt. However, critics cannot agree on whether or not she was the model for this piece. Although this is not one of Rembrandt's finer works, it is still effective genre painting.

PLATE 29

The Holy Family with Angels, painted in 1645, is one of Rembrandt's warmest and tenderest pieces. It is almost as if he were showing the viewer his envy of happy family life.

The setting itself has been shifted in time. With the exception of the angels, this is a seventeenth century Dutch family. A very relaxed feeling pervades the work. Instead of emphasizing the spiritual nature of the scene, Rembrandt has stressed tenderness. If the angels were removed, there would be nothing left in the painting to indicate that this is not a typical Dutch family.

PLATE 30

Rembrandt painted *The Holy Family with the Curtain* one year after he created *The Holy Family with Angels* (plate 29). Both paintings are set in seventeenth century Holland. As in the earlier painting, *The Holy Family with the Curtain* emphasizes domestic tranquility rather than spirituality. In fact, the second painting proceeds further in this direction, for the angels present in the earlier work are absent here. Mother and Child are caught in a moment of private tenderness, the father works in the background shadow, while the cat toasts itself in front of the fire.

This is a picture within a picture. The scene is surrounded by a painted frame that is in turn partially covered by a curtain. The device of the curtain seems strange to twentieth century viewers. However, placing a curtain in front of paintings was a seventeenth century Dutch custom.

PLATE 31

The small painting, *Winter Landscape,* is one of Rembrandt's best landscapes. The harshness of the scene heightens the realism. The people who inhabit this landscape appear strangely solitary. They seem to have more in common with their surroundings than with each other.

PLATE 32

In his mature religious works, Rembrandt was less dramatic than in his earlier religious paintings. This is particularly true of *Hannah and Samuel.* The artist has used light and color to help develop human character. Thus, the prophetess gazes into the distance. Her troubled face reveals her concern.

PLATE 33

The many self-portraits that Rembrandt painted constitute a visual record of his physical and mental aging. By 1650, when this *Self-Portrait* was painted, the artist was a middle-aged man of forty-four. When compared with his earlier self-portraits, the aging process is obvious. However, there has been another change. The cockiness and flamboyance have been replaced by a deep skepticism. In 1642, Rembrandt had been at the apex of his commercial appeal. During the years between 1642 and 1650, his popularity as an artist had begun to wane.

PLATE 34

The Mill, executed in about 1650, is the subject of much controversy among art scholars. The question of whether or not Rembrandt actually painted the piece has bothered scholars for some time. During the last two centuries, *The Mill* had a significant influence on many artists. The solitary mill, the small figures in the foreground, and the amazing use of chiaroscuro (the interplay of light and dark) give the piece a brooding, melancholy quality.

PLATE 35

By the 1650's, Rembrandt was no longer in such demand as a portrait painter. Although he still received commissions, the number of requests was considerably reduced. This was due to Rembrandt's changing style and interest. Just as his religious paintings were more character studies than theatrical stories, his portraits tended to be explorations into the subject's personality and character. Unfortunately, the general public preferred the flattering work of his youth.

This *Portrait of Clement de Jonghe* is typical of the sort of portrait the artist produced during the 1650's. The lighting helps establish an introspective, thoughtful quality.

PLATE 36

Rembrandt was a master at turning a small private moment into a beautiful work of art. In *Young Woman at Her Mirror,* the artist has captured such a moment. The woman's concentration is complete. This is more than a woman posing, it is a piece of life.

When it suited his artistic purpose, Rembrandt was capable of executing details in a way few other artists have ever matched. The woman's costume and jewelry are perfect examples of this ability.

PLATE 37

Jan Six was one of Rembrandt's most loyal patrons and supporters. Despite the fact the public's tastes and Rembrandt's style were in dramatic opposition, Six continued to support Rembrandt's art. This *Portrait of Jan Six,* painted in 1654, is one of the artist's finest portraits. The profound characterization shows a man of the world who was also deeply introspective. Both sides of the man's personality are seen in the red cloak and the predominant gray of the background and costume.

A few years after this piece was painted, Six abandoned Rembrandt. The split is said to have been the result of an unpaid debt.

PLATE 38

The Slaughtered Ox, painted in 1655, was the second version of a work created approximately fifteen years earlier. The piece shows Rembrandt's skill with still life. Yet, just as he usually included people in his landscapes, *The Slaughtered Ox* is not without company. A woman peers out from a doorway. The rendering of the ox is almost abstract in this version.

PLATE 39

In 1655, Rembrandt received a commission for three paintings. *Man in Armour* is one of these works. It is thought to be a portrait of Alexander the Great. At the time it was delivered, the buyer was dissatisfied with its size. Rembrandt added two canvas strips to enlarge the work. The artist and his sponsor continued to argue about the painting. Rembrandt, although by then in serious financial trouble, stubbornly refused to change it again.

PLATE 40

The drawing, *Woman Looking out of a Window,* shows one of Rembrandt's favorite poses. Several of his works incorporate people at windows, including the beautiful *Young Girl Leaning on a Windowsill* (plate 27). This type of genre work was much admired in Holland at the time. Although it is not known for sure, the model for this drawing might have been Hendrickje.

PLATE 41

The Anatomy Lesson of Dr. Joan Deyman was commissioned to honor the first dissection by the new head of the medical school. Unfortunately, the painting was severely damaged in a fire and only a fragment remains. However, a small drawing exists which indicates the original composition. In addition to the man on the left, there were seven other onlookers.

The placement of the corpse, feet facing the viewer and dramatically foreshortened, resembles Mantegna's *The Dead Christ.* It is known that the dissection was performed on the corpse of Joris Fonteyn, a man who had been hanged for thievery.

Dr. Deyman, having completed the dissection of the abdominal cavity, is shown dissecting the brain. The figure on the left appears to be holding the top of the skull.

PLATE 42

The portrait of *Hendrickje Stoffels Leaning Against a Door* was painted between 1656 and 1657. By this time, Rembrandt was bankrupt. Hendrickje and the artist's son rescued him by forming a corporation and hiring Rembrandt as an employee, freeing the artist from financial worries.

PLATE 43

As his fortunes changed, Rembrandt often relied on his neighborhood friends as models. Many of these neighbors were Jews. *Bearded Man in a Cap,* also known as *A Jewish Rabbi,* was painted at about the same time as the portrait of *Hendrickje Stoffels Leaning Against a Door* (plate 42). This is one of Rembrandt's finest portraits. The distant gaze and melancholy air are Rembrandt trademarks found in his mature works.

PLATE 44

Few other artists have painted as many self-portraits as Rembrandt did. None of the others has been able to use this form of expression as skillfully. Rembrandt's self-portraits are almost a diary. This *Self-Portrait,* painted in 1659, shows the artist at fifty-three. It is the face of a man who has gone through a very difficult period. No longer the master of his own finances, he faces the world with sorrow, but determination.

PLATE 45

In the early 1660's, Rembrandt painted *Woman Holding an Ostrich Feather.* A companion piece, known as *Man Holding Gloves,* was painted at the same time. This detail of the woman's face gives the viewer an opportunity to examine her hair and jewelry as well as the marvelous treatment of her eyes. The eyes and the lighting produce a depth of character that is truly exceptional. The woman's gaze is unfathomable. The trace of melancholy only adds to her dignity.

PLATE 46

There is some confusion regarding the dating of *Two Negroes.* The best explanation is that Rembrandt used the same models twice. The earlier version was completed in about 1656. This later version was painted in 1661. Blacks had appeared in paintings since the Renaissance. However, no other artist painted them so sensitively.

PLATE 47

St. Matthew the Evangelist, painted in 1661, is one of a series Rembrandt executed involving the apostles. The series was created during the early 1660's. It is not known for sure if the series had been commissioned or if it was painted for the artist himself.

St. Matthew the Evangelist is one of the most touching of the works from this series. Rembrandt shows Matthew deep in thought, pausing to consider his next words. Unnoticed by him, an angel whispers in his ear, providing the inspiration he seeks. The apostle's age is reflected in his worn face and knobby hands. This produces a sharp contrast with the youthful angel.

PLATE 48

As part of his series on the apostles, Rembrandt painted this *Self-Portrait as the Apostle Paul.* Like *St. Matthew the Evangelist* (plate 47), it was painted in 1661. It is interesting that the artist chose to picture himself as St. Paul. Perhaps Rembrandt identified himself with the apostle's conversion and ultimate martyrdom. The facial expression is difficult to describe. Is the artist asking a question, or showing that he knows the answer? Although the expression is a mystery, it elicits tremendous sympathy from the viewer. As was the case with Rembrandt's mature works, the piece compels the viewer to examine himself as well as the work of art.

Plate 1 The Angel and the Prophet Balaam, 1626, oil on panel, 25⅝″ X 18½″,
Musée Cognacq-Jay, Paris

Plate 2 Tobit and Anna with the Kid, 1626, oil on panel, 15½″ X 11¾″,
Rijksmuseum, Amsterdam, on loan from private collection

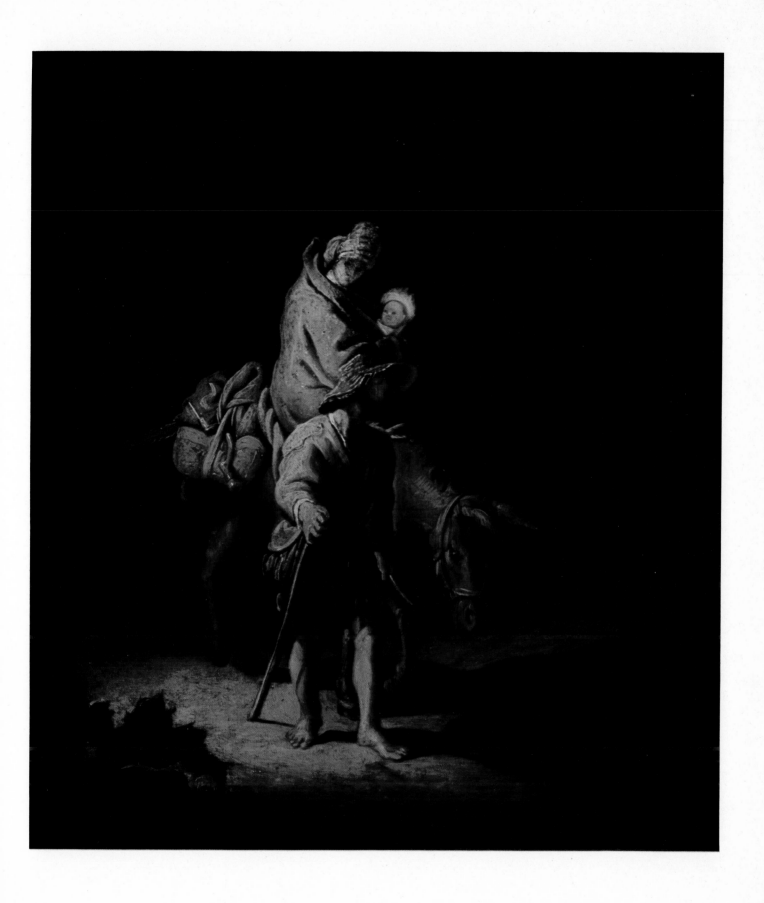

Plate 3 Flight into Egypt, c. 1625-26, oil on panel, 10½'' X 9¾'',
Musée des Beaux-Arts, Tours

Plate 4 St. Paul in Prison, 1627, oil on panel, 28⅝″ X 23¾″,
Staatsgalerie, Stuttgart

Plate 5 Self-Portrait, c. 1628, oil on panel, 8⅞″ X 7½″, Rijksmuseum, Amsterdam, on loan from private collection

Plate 6 Christ at Emmaus, c. 1629, oil on paper mounted on panel,
15⅜″ X 16½″, Musée Jacquemart-André,
Institute de France, Paris

Plate 7 Self-Portrait, c. 1629, oil on panel, 14¾″ X 11⅜″, Royal Cabinet of
Paintings, Mauritshuis, The Hague

Plate 8 The Tribute Money, 1629, oil on panel, 16⅛″ X 13″,
National Gallery, Toronto

Plate 9 Self-Portrait, 1629, oil on panel, 2′ 11″ X 2′ 5⅛″,
Isabella Stewart Gardner Museum, Boston

Plate 10 Jeremiah Contemplating the Destruction of Jerusalem, 1630,
oil on panel, 22⅞″ X 18½″, Rijksmuseum, Amsterdam

Plate 11 Portrait of Maurits Huygens, 1632, oil on panel,
12¼″ X 9¾″, Kunsthalle, Hamburg   27

Plate 12 The Artist's Sister, 1632, oil on panel, 21⅝'' X 18⅞'',
Brera Museum, Milan

Plate 13 Portrait of Maarten Looten, 1632, oil on panel, 3′ X 2′ 5½″,
County Museum of Art, Los Angeles

Plate 14 Saskia van Uhlenburgh, Wife of the Artist, 1633-35, oil on panel,
23¾″ X 19½″, National Gallery of Art, Washington, D.C.

Plate 15 Portrait of the Reverend Johannes Elison, 1634, oil on canvas,
5′ 8⅛″ X 4′ ⅞″, Museum of Fine Arts, Boston

Plate 16 Self-Portrait, 1634, oil on panel, 24⅝″ X 18½″, Mauritshuis, The Hague

Plate 17 Rembrandt and Saskia, 1636, oil on canvas, 5′ 3⅜′′ X 4′ 3½′′,
Gemäldegalerie, Staatliche Kunstsammlungen, Dresden   33

Plate 18 Landscape with the Baptism of the Chamberlain, 1636,
oil on canvas, 2′ 11⅝″ X 3′ 6½″, Landsmuseum, Hanover

Plate 19 The Sacrifice of Isaac, 1636, oil on canvas, 6′ 4¾′′ X 4′ 4′′,
Alte Pinakothek, Munich

Plate 20 Joseph Relating His Dreams, 1637, paper, grisaille, 20⅛″ X 15⅜″,
Rijksmuseum, Amsterdam

Plate 21 **Samson's Wedding Feast,** 1638, oil on canvas, 4′ 1¾″ X 5′ 9⅛″,
Gemäldegalerie, Staatliche Kunstsammlungen, Dresden

Plate 22 Portrait of Maria Trip, 1639, oil on panel, 3′ 6⅛″ X 2′ 8¼″,
Rijksmuseum, Amsterdam

Plate 23 The Meeting Between Mary and Elizabeth, 1640, oil on panel,
22¼″ X 18⅞″, Detroit Institute of Arts, Detroit

Plate 24 Manoah's Sacrifice, 1641, oil on canvas, 8′ ½″ X 9′ 5″, Gemäldegalerie,
Staatliche Museen, Dresden

Plate 25 Portrait of a Man, 1641, oil on canvas, 3′ 5½′′ X 2′ 8¾′′,
Royal Museum, Brussels

Plate 26 Hendrickje Stoffels, 1645, oil on canvas, 28⅜″ X 23⅝″, Louvre, Paris

Plate 27 Young Girl Leaning on a Windowsill, 1645, oil on canvas,
2′ 8⅛″ X 2′ 2″, Dulwich College Gallery, London   43

Plate 28 Woman in Bed, c. 1645-50, oil on canvas, 2′ 7⅞″ X 2′ 2⅜″,
National Gallery of Scotland, Edinburgh

Plate 29 The Holy Family with Angels, 1645, oil on canvas, 3′ 10″ X 2′ 11¾″,
Hermitage, Leningrad

Plate 30 The Holy Family with the Curtain, 1646, oil on panel, 18¼″ X 27″,
Staatliche Kunstsammlungen, Kassel

Plate 31 Winter Landscape, 1646, oil on panel, 6¼'' X 8⅝'',
Staatliche Kunstsammlungen, Kassel

Plate 32 Hannah and Samuel, 1648, oil on panel, 15⅞″ X 12½″,
National Gallery of Scotland, Edinburgh

Plate 33 Self-Portrait, 1650, oil on canvas, 3′ ¼″ X 2′ 5¾″,
National Gallery of Art, Washington, D. C.

Plate 34 The Mill, c. 1650, oil on canvas, 2′ 10½″ X 3′ 5½″,
National Gallery of Art, Washington, D. C.

Plate 35 Portrait of Clement de Jonghe; 1652-55, oil on canvas,
3′ 1″ X 2′ 5½″, private collection

Plate 36 Young Woman at Her Mirror, 1654, oil on panel,
16″ X 13″, Hermitage, Leningrad

Plate 37 Portrait of Jan Six, 1654, oil on canvas, 3′ 8″ X 3′ 4¼″,
Six Collection, Amsterdam

Plate 38 The Slaughtered Ox, 1655, oil on panel, 3′ 1″ X 2′ 2⅜″, Louvre, Paris

Plate 39 Man in Armour, 1655, oil on canvas, 4′ 6⅛″ X 3′ 5⅛″,
Art Gallery and Museum, Glasgow

Plate 40 Woman Looking out of a Window, c. 1655-56, drawing with
pen and brush in bistre, 11½″ X 6⅜″, Louvre, Paris

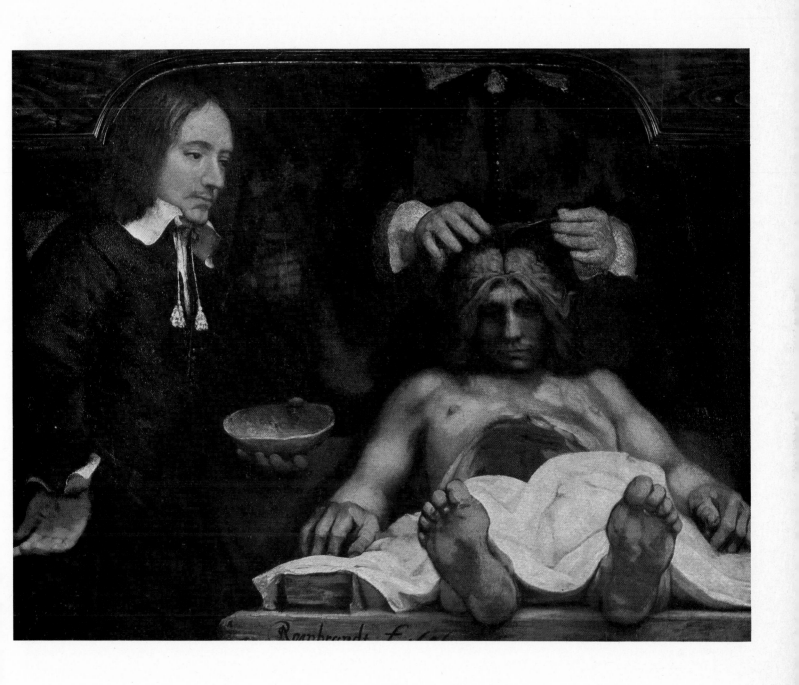

Plate 41 The Anatomy Lesson of Dr. Joan Deyman, 1656, oil on canvas,
3′ 3⅜″ X 4′ 4¾″, Rijksmuseum, Amsterdam

Plate 42 Hendrickje Stoffels Leaning Against A Door, c. 1656-57, oil on canvas,
2′ 10″ X 2′ 1½″, Gemäldegalerie, Staatliche Museen, Berlin-Dahlem

Plate 43 Bearded Man in a Cap, c. 1656-57, oil on canvas, 2′ 5⅝″ X 2′ 1¾″,
National Gallery, London

Plate 44 Self-Portrait, 1659, oil on canvas, 2′ 9¼″ X 2′ 2″,
National Gallery of Art, Washington, D. C.

Plate 45 Woman Holding an Ostrich Feather, detail—her face, c. 1660,
oil on canvas, National Gallery of Art, Washington, D. C.

61

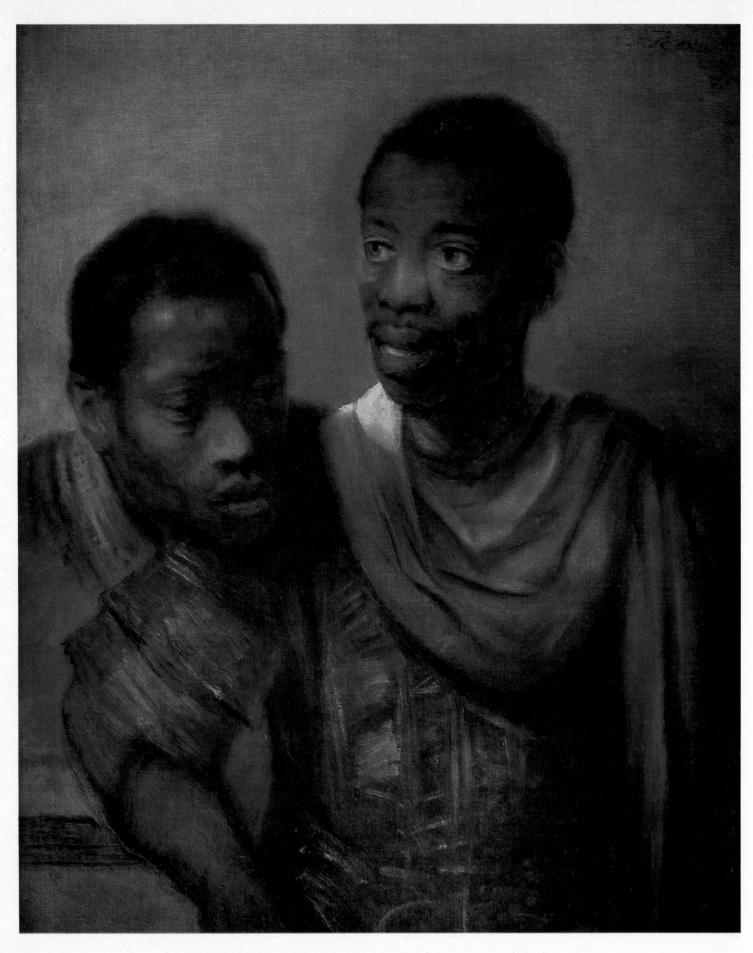

Plate 46 Two Negroes, 1661, oil on canvas, 2′ 6½″ X 2′ 1½″,
Mauritshuis, The Hague

Plate 47 St. Matthew the Evangelist, 1661, oil on canvas,
3′ 1¾″ X 2′ 7⅞″, Louvre, Paris

Plate 48 Self-Portrait as the Apostle Paul, 1661, oil on canvas, 2′ 11¾″ X 2′ 6¼″,
Rijksmuseum, Amsterdam